P9-BTO-892

STRESS Can Really Get on Your NERVES!

by Trevor Romain
& Elizabeth Verdick

free spirit
PUBLiSHiNG®

Works
for kids®

Library of Congress Cataloging-in-Publication Data
Romain, Trevor.
    Stress can really get on your nerves / by Trevor Romain & Elizabeth Verdick.
       p. cm.
    Summary: Uses silly jokes and light-hearted cartoons along with serious advice to help readers recognize the causes of stress and its effects and learn how to handle worry, anxiety, and stress.
    ISBN 1-57542-078-3 (pbk.)
    1. Stress in children—Juvenile literature. 2. Stress management for children—Juvenile literature. 3. Stress in adolescence—Juvenile literature. 4. Stress management for teenagers—Juvenile literature. [1. Stress (Psychology)] I. Verdick, Elizabeth. II. Title.

BF723.S75 R66 2000
155.9'042—dc21

                                  00-022614

10 9 8 7 6 5 4
Printed in Canada

Free Spirit Publishing Inc.
217 Fifth Avenue North, Suite 200
Minneapolis, MN 55401-1299
(612) 338-2068
help4kids@freespirit.com
www.freespirit.com

Dedication

This book is dedicated to our families who, with their loving support, helped us not to stress out while putting it together.

Acknowledgments

We'd like to extend a special thank you to teacher Alice Hansbarger, M.Ed., for sharing information about stressed-out students and how to help.

Contents

Introduction (Test Your Stress)

Before you read the rest of the book, take this test. It's fun! And you automatically get an A just for answering the questions.

1. At night, do you have dreams about getting chased, taking a test where you don't know any answers, or standing in front of a bunch of people without your clothes on? **Yes** or **No**

2. Does the thought of going to school ever worry you so much you could almost puke? **Yes** or **No**

3. Does your head sometimes feel like it's being squeezed by a boa constrictor? **Yes** or **No**

4. Some days, do you walk around so tired that you feel like you're on automatic pilot? **Yes** or **No**

5. Does your list of things to do seem a mile long? **Yes** or **No**

6. Do you ever wish for a magic wand to make your stress disappear? **Yes** or **No**

7. Are you often so tense that your shoulders are up to your ears? **Yes** or **No**

8. Would a good nickname for you be "Grouchy"? **Yes** or **No**

9. Are you sometimes as jumpy as a rubber ball bouncing off the ceiling? **Yes** or **No**

Boing!

10. Do you wish for aliens to capture you, so you could escape from your problems? **Yes** or **No**

11. Does the world ever seem to be spinning so fast that you want to get off for a moment and take a break? **Yes** or **No**

Your Score

If you answered **yes** to all or most of these questions, you are *stressed out* and this book can help.

If you answered **yes** to some of the questions, you can use this book to deal with stressful days.

If you answered **no** to all of the questions, you weren't telling the truth. Go stand in the corner.

(Just kidding!)

What in the World Is Stress?

Something you can't see or touch but definitely can feel.

The name for tension in your mind and body. A . . .

Reaction to things that are new, scary, or different. It's . . .

Especially common in kids who are shy or want to be "the best." A . . .

Source of headaches and stomachaches, it's also . . .

Something lots of kids don't even know they have!

Here are other ways to describe how you feel
when you're stressed:

all ALONE

anxious

burned out

confused

crabby

cranky

edgy

excited

fidgety

freaked OUT

frustrated

goose-bumpy

jittery

JUMPY

mixed up

moody

nervous

overwhelmed

panicky

pressured

queasy

ready to BURST

restless

scared

shaky

tense

tired out

trapped

troubled

upset

uptight

WIRED

worried

wound up

Different Types of Stress

Sometimes stress hits you all at once, like someone has just poured a bucket of water over your head. But sometimes stress is sneaky. It slowly creeps up, and you sense something's wrong but you don't know what it is.

Then there's the stress that just won't go away. It's been around so long that it's almost like a member of the family.

Stress takes its job *verrrrrrry* seriously. Look what it's responsible for:

STRESS's JOB DESCRIPTION

- Keep kids up all night with worry.

- Make them wake up tired and tense.

- Give them a sick feeling in their stomach and head.

- Cause them to feel sad, angry, helpless, alone, or upset.

- Make them anxious about life.

- Make it harder for them to do well in school, have fun, or try new activities.

- Get kids to scream and yell, or take out their feelings on other people.

- Make them want to run and hide.

- Convince them there's no such word as *relax*.

A Few Facts About Stress

You can't wish stress away or pretend it's not there. Stress doesn't like to be ignored.

(No wonder it can *really* get on your nerves.)

Stress isn't your mom or dad. You don't always have to do what it tells you!

And stress isn't a subject you *have* to take at school.

Stress can be measured in levels. How stressed are you right now?

THE STRESS-O-METER

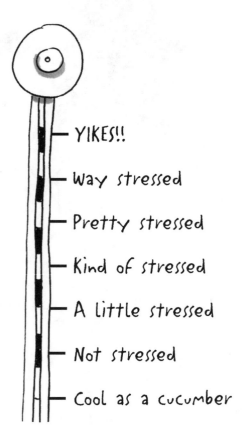

YIKES!!

Way stressed

Pretty stressed

Kind of stressed

A little stressed

Not stressed

Cool as a cucumber

A little stress isn't bad. In fact, sometimes you might feel excited or energized by it. For example, knowing your homework is due gives you that extra push you need to get it done. Feeling pumped up about your soccer match can help you play better. And realizing that your violin recital will take place soon might help you feel more eager to practice.

But being stressed most of the time can wear you down and make you sick—and turn you into a worried wreck.

Stress in Action

Stress sets off alarms in your brain and body. The moment you sense something stressful: **BEEP BEEP BEEP BEEP!** Instantly your reaction is to fight or run away.

Experts call this the "fight-or-flight response." This reaction has helped humans survive for millions of years.

Imagine yourself as a prehistoric person. There you are, innocently sharpening your spear, when from nowhere a hungry saber-toothed tiger jumps out from behind a bush!

If you just stood there doing nothing, you'd be . . .

DEAD MEAT.

Lucky for you, your body and brain automatically know what to do. In a flash, your "fight-or-flight response" kicks in:

- Your heart beats harder and faster, so you can run or defend yourself.

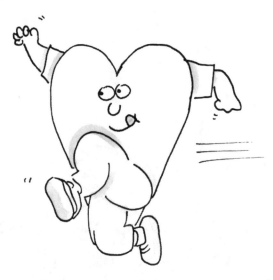

- The blood rushes to your large muscles (the ones that help you flee or fight).

- Your body makes chemicals like adrenaline, which boost your energy.

- You start to sweat as your body gets ready to run or fight.

- Your stomach shuts down, so your blood can flow where it's needed most.

All of this happens so you can face that hungry tiger or run away—and live to tell the story.

Now flash forward to the present. This time, it's not a hungry tiger you're dealing with, but a deadly dangerous . . .

ORAL REPORT!

You stand up in front of the class, and—quick as lightning—your "fight-or-flight response" turns on. The following reactions may take place:

These reactions aren't exactly helpful in this situation!

Times have changed, but people's reactions to danger or stress are as strong as ever. To prove it, try this: Right now, close your eyes and imagine you're walking down a dark street all alone when suddenly you hear footsteps behind you. Feel a little nervous? Just thinking about a tense situation can set off your alarms.

Sources of Stress

Lots of things can cause stress in kids' lives. Here are a few:

homework

tests

school

team tryouts

busy schedules

fights with friends

bullies

fears about violence

worrying about what's
happening in the world

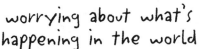

grades

family troubles

wanting to be
liked by others

Do you sometimes feel anxious about some of
these things? If you do, you're not alone.

You may also feel stressed if your after-school time looks like this:

Soccer
1

Study group
2

Dog-sitting job
3

Having lots of activities can help you become a well-rounded person. *Too many* can make you a *worn-out* person. Let your mom or dad know if you're overloaded. Which activities can you cut down on?

⑥ Homework— and plenty of it

⑤ Play rehearsal

④ Visit best friend

When you're tense, you may feel like shouting at someone or escaping. Neither one will make your stress go away. Stress comes right back—like a boomerang. **LOOK OUT!**

Strange-But-True Tales

Stress can make *anyone* worried, nervous, and upset. (Even grown-ups.) When you feel this way, it's natural to want to run for the nearest exit. Plenty of kids have tried to do just that. Read on. . . .

Rosa* was nervous about playing volleyball in front of the other kids. She thought she'd miss the ball and everyone would yell at her. To get out of the game, she asked a friend to help create a fake bruise with makeup. When they were done, Rosa showed her newly black-and-blue finger (and not-too-real-looking bandage) to the gym teacher—who wasn't exactly fooled!

*These stressed-out kids are real—their names aren't.

When Jarvis was at summer camp for the first time, he didn't want to admit he was anxious about being away from his family. He got so stressed out that he started to feel sick. In the nurse's office, he wrote long letters to his parents, begging to come home. He even tried to raise his temperature by lying under a bunch of blankets in the summer heat. But Jarvis didn't get sent home—and he spent most of camp in bed.

Brian had had enough. His mom kept pressuring him to clean his room, do his homework, practice his clarinet, be nice to his sister, feed the fish, make better grades, be on time for school, and do his chores without being asked. He couldn't take it anymore, so one night he shouted at the top of his lungs, **"I'M MOVING OUT AND YOU'LL NEVER SEE ME AGAIN!!"** He packed a suitcase and walked out the door. But it was dark and scary outside. After standing on the driveway for ten minutes, he decided to go back in.

Lexy was one of the fastest runners in school. One day during gym, the class went outside for the 100-yard dash. She wanted to win more than anything. But right before the race, Lexy got nervous and felt too scared to compete. She pretended to hurt her ankle and then faked a limp. In the excitement of watching the races, she forgot what she was doing. Some of the other kids noticed and called out:

She said she hurt her LEFT ankle, but she's limping on her RIGHT!

Maybe you've tried to get out of stressful situations by running away or faking being sick or hurt. For example, have you ever pretended to be ill on a day you had a test? (This is pretty common for kids to do.) Maybe you stayed in bed watching TV instead of going to school. You escaped—what a relief! Or *did* you? You eventually had to take that test. And while you were studying for it later, you may have fallen behind in your other work, causing even more tension. Avoiding the things you need to do doesn't actually help you avoid stress.

Escape Plans Guaranteed to Backfire!

1. Skipping school. Not a good idea. Sooner or later, you get caught—and detention is no fun.

2. Using food as an escape. Candy, doughnuts, chips, and fast food are more tempting during stressful times. But eating lots of sugary, salty treats puts more stress on your body.

3. Using drugs and alcohol. Getting drunk or high doesn't solve problems—it creates *more*.

What can you do instead of trying to escape?
Put your worries into words. Talk about what's
bothering you. Good places to go for help include
parents, relatives, teachers, school counselors,
a youth group leader, a religious advisor, your
family doctor, or your principal. You can say,
"I'm really stressed out, and I don't know what
to do. Can you help me?"

A Few More Not-So-Great Escapes

This may come as a surprise, but some of the things you do to relax can actually make you more stressed!

video games

computer games

television

The World's Worst Stress Relievers*

Bumping your head against a wall won't help you feel less stressed. All this will do is give you a large lump and a bad headache.

*Warning: Don't try these. Seriously!

Breaking things won't reduce your stress level either. If your stuff is broken, this will annoy you even more.

Kicking bricks will only hurt your foot!

Blaming everything and everyone but yourself doesn't get you very far.

Swearing won't get you anywhere but in trouble!

Taking out your stress on an animal is hurtful—to both of you. Your pet doesn't understand the word *stress*. All a pet wants is love.

Stuffing your noisy little brother in the closet will **NOT** reduce your stress. (If you're busy and a brother or sister is bugging you, talk to your parents.)

NO!!! Cigarettes *don't* help you feel relaxed and refreshed! Smoking is more like standing in a smelly cloud of truck exhaust while licking an old rubber tire.

When you're stressed out, wound up, freaked out, or fed up, it's time to **CHILL OUT.** You have the power to put stress in its place. All you need are the right tools.

How to Be a Panic Mechanic

A mechanic fixes your car. A Panic Mechanic fixes your stress. (This is very different from a Manic Mechanic—who only makes things worse!)

If you're stressed out, you can become your own Panic Mechanic—which means you look at what's wrong (your Stress Mess) and use your tools to make repairs.

Stress Mess #1: You're restless, frantic, and jumpy as a frog.

Help yourself level out.

Stress produces lots of extra energy in your body. Do something positive with it! Run with your dog or go skateboarding, for example. If you're jittery at school, ask your teacher if you can take a bathroom break. Walk quickly (but quietly) down the hall and do some stretches in the rest room.

Stress Mess #2: You're so stressed out, everything annoys you. Even a little noise or movement makes you want to scream.

Get quiet.

Take some time alone to calm down. Go to your bedroom or the basement, or make a secret hideaway using a table and some blankets. Put on some headphones. You may even enjoy closing your eyes and imagining you're somewhere very peaceful: a tree house, a quiet beach, or outside during a snowfall.

Stress Mess #3: When stressing out leads to spacing out.

Five minutes later:

Breathe deeply.

If you catch yourself zoning out in class or during conversations, take a few deep breaths. This brings oxygen to your brain and helps you think better. If possible, go outside for some fresh air.

Stress Mess #4: You worry almost all the time—even about things that aren't likely to happen.

All that worrying shows that you've got a good imagination! Use it to do something creative like draw, write a story, make up a dance, design a Web site, or work on a comedy routine. Focusing on something fun helps push the worries out of your mind.

Stress Mess #5: You feel like stress is the boss of your life.

You'd better do what I say!

Cut your stress down to size.

Stress can be overwhelming. You may feel like you can't handle things anymore. Don't push the panic button! *You* are bigger than your stress. Tell yourself that you're going to find ways to reduce your stress level.

For ideas, look at the Quick Fixes on pages 64–67.

Quick Fixes for Stressful Days

- Listen to soothing music.

- Relax with your friends.

- Go for a long walk.

- Play a musical instrument or do something artistic.

- Enjoy your hobby.

- Watch a movie—not a scary one!

- Read a good book.

- Practice deep breathing. Breathe in and imagine your breath is a wave: it comes in through your toes and washes up your body all the way to your head. As you breathe out, imagine the wave washing back down through your body, down to your toes, and out to sea. Do this a few times until you feel more peaceful.

- Volunteer your time. Helping someone else is a great way to help yourself!

- Do some chores. (It may sound crazy, but jobs like raking leaves or cleaning your room can actually help you calm down.)

- Make a worry jar. If you're a worrywart and your fears bother you all day long, set aside a special time to write your worries on little slips of paper. When you see them written out, their power begins to fade. Trap them in a jar where they can't bother you as much.

- Love your pet. It's a proven fact that animals can lower people's stress levels. Play with your dog, pet your cat, listen to your bird chirp, or watch your fish swim. These are great ways to relax.

Stress Mess #6: Stress makes you feel like your life is one **BIG** problem.

Look at each problem carefully.

When you're stressed, you have a general feeling that things aren't right in your life. You may lose sight of what was bothering you in the first place. Take some time to see the problem more clearly. Are you upset or worried about something in your life that's changed—or is about to change? Once you've spotted the problem, you can work on it.

Stress Mess #7: Worry makes you hurry.

Put on the brakes.

Moving too fast just gets you *more* anxious! And doing sixteen things at once can stress you to the max. (For example, don't try to do homework while eating dinner, talking on the phone, watching TV, and reading a magazine.) It's okay to do one thing at a time—and take your time doing it. Life doesn't have to be a race.

Stress Mess #8: You're so stressed about every-thing you have to do that you can't do *any* of it.

Make a to-do list.

Lots of people get stressed out because they're overwhelmed with all that they have to accomplish. Making a to-do list can help you feel less panicky. Start by listing all your tasks. Now rank them in order of importance. Does the first job on your list seem impossible? Break it down into chunks. Ready to tackle it? If not, break it down some more. *Now* does it seem possible? If it does, then complete the first task on your list. After that, take a break to reward yourself. Now you're ready for the next task!

Stress Mess #9: You're so stressed out that you feel tight and tense from head to toe.

Loosen the tension.

Stress leads to excess muscle tension, making you feel achy, stiff, or stretched to your limit. If you feel this way, try a relaxation exercise to loosen the tension. You'll find one starting on the next page.

Relax in 10 Easy Steps

This relaxation exercise is easy to learn. Read through the steps before you give it a try.

1. Find a quiet place where you won't be disturbed. (If possible, go outdoors—to the yard or to the park, for example. The fresh air will feel good.)

2. Lie down on the grass (or on the floor). Get comfortable.

3. Close your eyes, but don't fall asleep.

4. Breathe deeply. Focus on your breath going in and out. Count to five as you breathe in; count backwards from five as you breathe out. Take your time.

5. When you feel calmer, continue the deep breathing, but as you breathe out, say the word *relax* in your mind.

6. In time with your breathing, begin to relax your muscles from head to toe. Start with your forehead. Tense those muscles as you breathe in, then relax them as you breathe out.

7. Continue tensing and relaxing—moving downward to your shoulders, arms, hands, stomach, legs, and feet. Each time, breathe in as you tense the muscles, and breathe out as you relax them.

8. Once you've reached your toes, take a rest. Keep breathing deeply.

9. Slowly open your eyes. You are now relaxed.

10. Enjoy this feeling!

You can do the exercise any time you want to feel calmer. Remember the "fight-or-flight response"? It has an opposite: **REST AND DIGEST.** This means your muscles are relaxed, your mind is clear, and your stomach is open for business again. Relaxation helps you get there!

Stress Mess #10: You're so frantic you're about ready to pop.

Get a grip on yourself.

Do you ever say things like, "If I don't make the team, I'll die!" or "I can't live without that pair of jeans!" Will these things actually kill you? Of course not! Telling yourself, "I might feel disappointed if I don't get what I want" is more realistic—and less stressful. This is a great way to lighten a stressful load.

Stress Mess #11: You feel like a big loser all the time.

Brighten your outlook.

What could be more stressful than constantly telling yourself what a loser you are? If a little voice in your head is always putting you down, tell that voice to take a hike! Instead of, "Everyone will think I'm a dork" and "I'll just make a mess of it if I try," you can tell yourself, "I'm working hard and improving" and "Everyone makes mistakes sometimes."

Stress Mess #12: It seems like your life is spinning totally out of control.

Use your safety net.

It's not just tightrope walkers who need safety nets. At some point, *everybody* needs someone to catch them when they're falling. Who do you trust with your problems? Who's a good listener and advice-giver? Find those people and ask for some help.

Daily Ways to Keep Stress at Bay

1. **Be active.** Exercise does more than build up your body—it also lifts your spirits and helps you feel more relaxed. When you're active, you become stronger in your body and your mind. And that means you've got more power over stress.

2. **Eat right.** Eating food that's good for your body helps you stay healthy—and a healthy body is a better stress-fighter. Eat plenty of fruits, vegetables, whole grains, dairy products, and lean meats.

3. **Avoid caffeine.** This chemical—found mainly in drinks like soda, coffee, and tea—can make you feel edgy and tense. (It's like you ingest some stress!)

4. **Get enough sleep each night.** It's hard to deal with stress if you're feeling tired and run down.

During a good night's sleep, your mind and body recharge. This means you're sharper and stronger when you wake up.

5. **Express your feelings.** Are you angry, sad, frustrated, jealous, hurt, or upset? Talk to someone or write about it. Locking up your feelings can add to your stress.

6. **Laugh it up.** Experts say laughter reduces stress. So memorize some jokes, read the funnies, or see a comedy. Giggling is good for you!

7. **Be neat.** Do you have trouble remembering where you put your stuff? Kids' rooms are famous for swallowing things like trading cards, party invitations, homework, secret notes—even the occasional peanut butter sandwich. Losing stuff can stress you out. Keeping your room clean and organized helps a lot.

8. **Be a planner.** Feeling overwhelmed? Like you're behind in everything? Time for some planning. Get a calendar and write down your projects, test dates, and other important stuff. Now make a homework and study schedule you can follow. A little advance planning will help you feel more in control of your days.

9. **Talk about your problems.** Who's a caring and trusted listener—your mom, your dad, your teacher, your best friend? Talk to that person. Share your problems. You'll feel better if you do.

10. **Forgive your own mistakes.** Are you really hard on yourself every time you make a mistake? Beating yourself up over errors never helps. Instead, tell yourself that mistakes are learning experiences. (At least you know what *not* to do next time.)

11. **Be yourself.** Trying to be something you're not just to keep up with the "cool" people can cause a lot of stress. Is there a better way? Sure! Simply being *you*—and being happy with your own style of cool.

12. **Feel good about what you have.** Wanting expensive clothes and other stuff you can't afford can leave you feeling like you never have enough. Instead of thinking about everything you *want*, take a moment to think about everything you already *have*. Make a list of what you're grateful for. You may quickly

see that some of the best things in life don't cost money: a loving family, people who care about you, a dog licking your face, a sunny day.

Stress can really get on your nerves—but now you know what to do when it does. You can understand where stress comes from. You can be a Panic Mechanic and relieve much of the stress in your life. And no matter what's happening or how you feel, you can always take a deep breath and calm down. Stick to your stress-reducing plans, so stress won't get the best of you!

A Note for Parents and Teachers

In today's fast-paced, pressured world, more kids than ever are stressed out. But many don't know it—and neither do the adults in their lives. Many kids don't understand what stress is all about, and adults don't realize that kids can experience stress. They think it's a condition reserved for adults with grown-up responsibilities and obligations. They may not realize that the responsibilities and obligations of being a kid can weigh just as heavy and cause just as much anxiety.

Stress in kids often stays hidden. They may have symptoms of stress—headaches, stomachaches, trouble sleeping, lack of appetite—but because they don't know what stress is, they may think they're getting sick. And because many adults assume that kids can't experience stress, they may treat these symptoms as signs of physical illness—which doesn't "cure" them because it doesn't address the cause. *Tip: Stress symptoms in children are often physical.*

Some kids wonder if something is wrong with them—but they don't want to talk about it because they think no one will understand. And some kids who are coping with chronic stress have symptoms that are terribly embarrassing to them.

Examples:

- wanting to cry all the time
- being frightened of the world
- feeling scared of the dark and of strangers
- worrying that something terrible will happen
- wetting the bed
- not wanting to be alone
- having nightmares
- feeling helpless

What can you do to help kids deal with stress? Start by recognizing that stress is very real for kids— it can be a big part of their lives. Look for signs of hidden or "secret" stress. Are there physical symptoms? Is their school performance suffering? What about their relationships with friends and family? When stress starts affecting kids'  everyday lives, this gives them even *more* to worry about and makes them feel *more* stressed. Caring, aware adults can break this cycle.

Here are specific things you can do to help kids with their stress:

- Provide them with a safe, familiar, consistent environment.
- Make sure they have a dependable routine.
- Encourage them to talk openly about feelings and problems.
- Listen if they confide their worries or fears.
- Offer affection, never criticism, if they express anxiety.
- Become more aware of the causes of their stress (new experiences, fear of failure, change, loss).
- Talk about upcoming changes and challenges in their lives.
- Spend time being calm and relaxed together.
- Make sure they're physically active and eat healthy foods.
- Encourage them to get enough sleep.
- Help them prepare the night before, so mornings aren't too rushed.
- Give them a chance to make choices, so they have some control over their lives.
- Help them build their self-esteem by encouraging them to be proud of who they are.

- Recognize and help build on strengths.
- Involve them in situations or activities where they have a good chance of succeeding.
- Ask yourself if your expectations of them are too high, leading to increased pressure in their lives.
- Seek professional help, if needed, by consulting a doctor, psychologist, counselor, or social worker.

Even young children can learn to recognize the signs of stress and begin resolving situations that are causing problems for them. Reading this book is a good first step. You might want to read it with your child (or your class) and allow time for questions and discussion.

For more information on kids and stress, take a look at this helpful book:

KidStress: What It Is, How It Feels, How to Help by Georgia Witkin, Ph.D. (New York: Viking Penguin, 1999). The author surveyed hundreds of kids and parents across the nation to find out what they had to say about stress. She provides excellent tips to figure out if children are overloaded, and offers ways you can help them—at any age and stage—to help themselves.

About the Authors

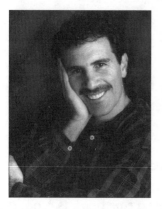

When South African-born **Trevor Romain** was 12, his teacher told him he wasn't talented enough to do art. By accident, he found out 20 years later that he could draw. Since that lucky day, he has written and illustrated 20 books for children. In addition to writing, Trevor regularly visits schools to speak to children, and he spends his free time with kids who have cancer at the Brackenridge Hospital in Austin, Texas.

Elizabeth Verdick is a children's book writer and editor. She has worked with Trevor on all of his books with Free Spirit Publishing and is the coauthor of *How to Take the GRRRR Out of Anger* (with Marjorie Lisovskis) and *Making Every Day Count* (with Pamela Espeland). Elizabeth lives in Minnesota with her husband, their two children, two cats, and a dog.

Other Great Books from Free Spirit

True or False? Tests Stink!
by Trevor Romain and Elizabeth Verdick

Tests are hard. Tests are scary. In fact, tests stink! This book has the answers to help kids do and be their best on test days. For ages 8–13.

$9.95; 88 pp.; softcover; illus.; 5⅛" x 7"

How to Do Homework Without Throwing Up
by Trevor Romain

Hilarious cartoons and witty insights teach important truths about homework and positive, practical strategies for getting it done. For ages 8–13.

$8.95; 72 pp.; softcover; illus.; 5⅛" x 7"

Bullies Are a Pain in the Brain *by Trevor Romain*
Every child needs to know how to cope with bullies. This book blends humor with practical suggestions to help kids become "Bully-Proof." For ages 8–13.

$9.95; 112 pp.; softcover; illus; 5⅛" x 7"

Cliques, Phonies, & Other Baloney *by Trevor Romain*
Written for every kid who has ever felt excluded or trapped by a clique, this book blends humor with practical advice as it tackles a serious subject. For ages 8–13.

$9.95; 136 pp.; softcover; illus.; 5⅛" x 7"

*To place an order or to request a free catalog of SELF-HELP FOR KIDS®
and SELF-HELP FOR TEENS® materials, please write, call, email,
or visit our Web site:*

Free Spirit Publishing Inc.
217 Fifth Avenue North • Suite 200• Minneapolis, MN 55401-1299
call toll-free 800.735.7323 • or locally 612.338.2068 • fax 612.337.5050
help4kids@freespirit.com • www.freespirit.com

Visit us on the Web!

www.freespirit.com

Stop by anytime to find our Parents' Choice Approved catalog with fast, easy, secure 24-hour online ordering; "Ask Our Authors," where visitors ask questions—and authors give answers—on topics important to children, teens, parents, teachers, and others who care about kids; links to other Web sites we know and recommend; fun stuff for everyone, including quick tips and strategies from our books; and much more! Plus our site is completely searchable so you can find what you need in a hurry. Stop in and let us know what you think!

Just point and click!

new! Get the first look at our books, catch the latest news from Free Spirit, and check out our site's newest features.

contact Do you have a question for us or for one of our authors? Send us an email. Whenever possible, you'll receive a response within 48 hours.

order! Order in confidence! Our secure server uses the most sophisticated online ordering technology available. And ordering online is just one of the ways to purchase our books: you can also order by phone, fax, or regular mail. No matter which method you choose, excellent service is our ultimate goal.

For a fast and easy way to receive our practical tips, helpful information, and special offers, send your email address to e-news@freespirit.com. View a sample letter and our privacy policy at *www.freespirit.com*.

1.800.735.7323 • fax 612.337.5050 • help4kids@freespirit.com